This book is in memory of
Sally Kissinger Wilt

GREAT CITIES
OF THE WORLD

LOS ANGELES

SABRINA CREWE

WORLD ALMANAC® LIBRARY

Please visit our web site at: www.worldalmanaclibrary.com
For a free color catalog describing World Almanac® Library's list of high-quality books
 and multimedia programs, call 1-800-848-2928 (USA) or 1-800-387-3178 (Canada).
World Almanac® Library's fax: (414) 332-3567.

Library of Congress Cataloging-in-Publication Data available upon request from publisher.
Fax (414) 336-0157 for the attention of the Publishing Records Department.

ISBN 0-8368-5029-7 (lib. bdg.)
ISBN 0-8368-5189-7 (softcover)

First published in 2004 by
World Almanac® Library
330 West Olive Street, Suite 100
Milwaukee, WI 53212 USA

Produced by Discovery Books
Editor: Helen Dwyer
Series designers: Laurie Shock, Keith Williams
Designer and page production: Keith Williams
Photo researcher: Rachel Tisdale
Maps and diagrams: Stefan Chabluk
World Almanac® Library editorial direction: Mark J. Sachner
World Almanac® Library editor: Jenette Donovan Guntly
World Almanac® Library art direction: Tammy Gruenewald
World Almanac® Library production: Jessica Morris

Photo credits: AKG-Images: p.15; Art Directors & Trip: pp.8, 24, 35, 38, 41, 42; Art Directors & Trip/Eric Smith:
p.37; Corbis: pp.12, 18, 25; Corbis/David Butow: p.29; Corbis/Jan Butchofsky-Houser: p.11; Corbis/Jim Sugar
Photography: pp.31, 40; Corbis/Joseph Sohm/ChromoSohm Inc.: pp.16, 20; Corbis/Peter Turnley: p.19; Corbis/
Richard Cummins: p.21; Corbis/Robert Holmes: p.36; Corbis/Robert Landau: p.23; Corbis/Roger Ressmeyer:
p.27; Corbis/Ted Soqui: p.39; David Simson – DASPHOTOGB@aol.com: p.32; Los Angeles County Metropolitan
Transportation Authority/Armando Arorizo: p.43; Mann's Theatres: p.7; North Wind Picture Archives: p.10; Port
of Los Angeles: p.30; Still Pictures/Alex Maclean: p.22; Still Pictures/Jim Wark: p.4

Cover caption: At night, the sky over downtown Los Angeles glows with light.

Printed in the United States of America

1 2 3 4 5 6 7 8 9 08 07 06 05 04

Contents

Introduction

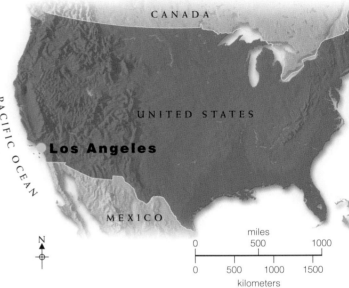

The nature of city life is that it is diverse. Most of the world's great cities have an ethnic mix, a lively culture, a contrast between wealth and poverty, and a colorful history. All of these factors determine what life is like for city dwellers.

Los Angeles, however, can truly claim to be one of the most diverse cities on Earth. Known for its endless sprawl of suburbs, the city also encompasses mountains, woodland, and beaches. It is famous as the capital of the movie industry and yet is hardly recognized as the United States' biggest and most important seaport. Some of the United States' most fabulous houses

◀ *The mountains surrounding Los Angeles can be seen from some of the city's taller buildings.*

*"This place did not seem like earth;
it was paradise."*

—Charlotte Perkins Gilman, 1890s.

contrast with homelessness and widespread poverty. The diversity also lies in the population—people of many races and cultures live in Los Angeles today.

A Coastal City

Los Angeles and its surrounding metropolitan area are situated along the coast of southern California. Most of the city is on the Los Angeles Plain, but its landscape ranges from beaches to hills and even includes mountains where the Santa Monica range enters the city. Los Angeles has another geographical feature that is not so pleasant: the San Andreas Fault and other lesser faults in the area are cracks in the Earth's crust that make the ground unstable and cause earthquakes. People in Los Angeles live with this ever-present threat.

The city has a warm and sunny climate, with an average daily high temperature of about 74° Fahrenheit (23.3° Celsius), although it can soar well over 100° F (37.7° C). The weather allows for an agreeable outdoor lifestyle that has attracted millions of people to the Los Angeles area.

*"This 'City of the Angels' is anything
else, unless the angels are fallen ones."*

—John W. Audubon, painter, 1849–50.

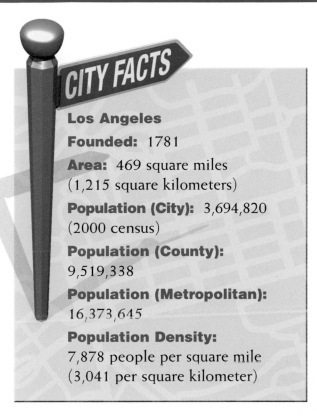

CITY FACTS

Los Angeles
Founded: 1781
Area: 469 square miles (1,215 square kilometers)
Population (City): 3,694,820 (2000 census)
Population (County): 9,519,338
Population (Metropolitan): 16,373,645
Population Density: 7,878 people per square mile (3,041 per square kilometer)

The City of the Angels

Los Angeles—Spanish for "the angels"—is often called just "L.A." At 469 square miles (1,215 square kilometers), it is the third largest city in the United States and has the second-largest population (after New York City). The city of Los Angeles comprises many distinct neighborhoods within six main areas: the San Fernando Valley, Westside, Downtown/Central, South Central, the Harbor, and the Beach/Airport area.

Changing Boundaries?

As the city sprawls and grows, some neighborhoods want to separate themselves and form their own cities. The San Fernando Valley has from time to time tried to secede from the city and in 2002, no fewer than seven areas of the city proposed

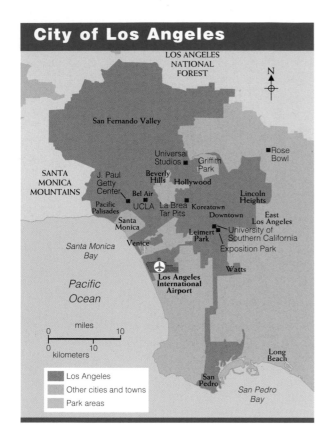

City of Los Angeles

LOS ANGELES NATIONAL FOREST

San Fernando Valley

SANTA MONICA MOUNTAINS

Universal Studios
Griffith Park
Rose Bowl

J. Paul Getty Center
Beverly Hills
Hollywood

Bel Air
Pacific Palisades
UCLA
La Brea Tar Pits
Koreatown
Lincoln Heights

Santa Monica
Downtown
East Los Angeles

Leimert Park
University of Southern California
Exposition Park

Venice

Santa Monica Bay

Watts

Pacific Ocean

Los Angeles International Airport

miles
0   10

0   10
kilometers

Long Beach

San Pedro
San Pedro Bay

Los Angeles
Other cities and towns
Park areas

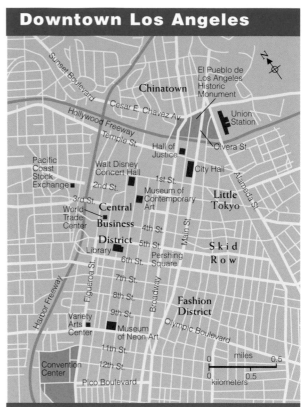

Downtown Los Angeles

Sunset Boulevard

Chinatown

El Pueblo de Los Angeles Historic Monument

Cesar E. Chavez Av.

Hollywood Freeway

Union Station

Temple St.

Olvera St.

Pacific Coast Stock Exchange

Hall of Justice

Walt Disney Concert Hall

City Hall

1st St.

2nd St.

Museum of Contemporary Art

Little Tokyo

3rd St.

World Trade Center

Central Business District

4th St.

Alameda St.

5th St.

Skid Row

Library

6th St.

Pershing Square

Main St.

Figueroa St.

7th St.

8th St.

Broadway

Fashion District

Harbor Freeway

Variety Arts Center

9th St.

Museum of Neon Art

Olympic Boulevard

11th St.

Convention Center

12th St.

Pico Boulevard

miles
0   0.5

0   0.5
kilometers

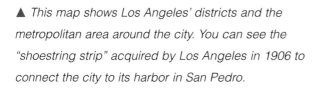

▲ This map shows Los Angeles' districts and the metropolitan area around the city. You can see the "shoestring strip" acquired by Los Angeles in 1906 to connect the city to its harbor in San Pedro.

seceding. Two of the proposals went to a vote: In 2002, Los Angeles' citizens voted on whether or not Hollywood and the San Fernando Valley should secede. The idea was not approved by the electorate, but residents have not given up. One day, the shape of Los Angeles still may change.

Los Angeles County, of which Los Angeles is the undisputed center, is the most populated in the United States. About 10 million people live there, mostly in the

"Wracked by floods, droughts, and earthquakes . . . . it doesn't matter; nothing is as outrageous as a dream, and a city founded on dreams and scorning prudence is likely to endure forever."

—Brendan Gill, architectural writer.

southern part of the county around the city. The larger metropolitan area around Los Angeles has spread to include several hundred cities and other communities. These suburbs are not just in Los Angeles County but also in the neighboring counties of Ventura, Orange, San Bernardino, and Riverside.

What Is Los Angeles?

What is and what is not part of the city of Los Angeles can be confusing. San Pedro and the Harbor, located to the south and connected only by a narrow corridor of land through Los Angeles County, are part of the city. Beverly Hills, right in the middle and surrounded by Los Angeles on all sides, is a city in its own right. Disneyland and Universal Studios, the two most famous tourist attractions associated with Los Angeles, are not in the city. The San Fernando Valley—a large chunk of Los Angeles comprising many neighborhoods—is part of Los Angeles, but many residents don't want it to be. East Los Angeles is an unincorporated community in Los Angeles County.

▲ *The Chinese Theater on Hollywood Boulevard opened in 1927. Modeled on a Chinese pagoda, it is a famous Los Angeles landmark, partly because of its front courtyard where movie stars have had their handprints and footprints embedded in cement.*

The Los Angeles metropolitan area, or Greater Los Angeles as it is also known, is one of the United States' industrial centers. Not only is it one of the top manufacturing regions, but it leads in many other industries, such as tourism, fashion, and science and technology. And, as the gateway to the countries of the Pacific Rim and Latin America, Los Angeles plays an increasingly important role in linking the United States to the rest of the world.

CHAPTER 1

History of Los Angeles

Some scientists say there were people living in the Los Angeles area fifty thousand years ago. Others disagree, but there is evidence of humans in the area at least twenty-five thousand years ago. In 1936, an amazing find was made in West Los Angeles when construction workers dug up part of a skull. Dated to 23,000 B.C., the remains of the so-called "Los Angeles Man" are among the oldest found on the continent.

La Brea Tar Pits

The La Brea Tar Pits in the heart of Los Angeles existed forty thousand years before there was a city on the spot. The black, bubbling bogs, still seeping asphalt out of the ground today, were the first indication to early settlers that there was oil in western North America. The site became even more interesting in 1875 when scientists began to find the fossilized remains of Ice Age animals that had become trapped in the tar. Over half a million specimens have now been recovered from the pits, and many—including the first saber-toothed tiger skull ever found—are on display at the museum at the La Brea Tar Pits.

◀ *Today, visitors to the La Brea Tar Pits can see models of prehistoric animals that once lived there.*

The Native People of California

About 8,000 B.C., the Chumash people began settling along the coast of what is now southern California. Much later, about A.D. 200–300, another Native American group, the Tongva, moved to the coast from inland and became the main group in the Los Angeles region.

A Spanish Colony

Everything changed for the Native Americans in the region when the Spanish arrived in the 1700s. Since the early 1500s, the Spanish had controlled land in South, Central, and North America, exploiting the Native people and natural resources. Their colony was called New Spain. Its center was in Mexico, but it included what are now California and the southwestern United States.

The Spanish did not settle in the California region until the mid-1700s, when Spain decided to found settlements there to keep control of its empire. Few colonists, however, were willing to come from Mexico to this faraway part of New Spain. So in 1769, groups of Catholic priests and Spanish soldiers were sent to found missions along the coast of California.

The California Missions

Two missions were founded in the Los Angeles area: San Gabriel Arcángel in 1771

Life in Native California

Like other coastal peoples in California, the Tongva and Chumash relied on the plentiful wild foods of the region. Not only did the sea provide abundant food, but the fertile land offered a wide range of plants and animals. An abundance of food and good land meant that life was much more peaceful in the Los Angeles region than in other parts of North America. People tended to live in small groups and had little need for the military and political alliances that formed among more warrior-like nations. There was a flourishing trade among the tribes of California and beyond, however, and the southern Californians traded fish and other seafood for items they wanted, such as woven baskets or types of rock that were good for making tools.

"After traveling about a league and a half through a pass between low hills we entered a very spacious valley, well grown with cottonwoods and alders, among which ran a beautiful river . . . . As soon as we arrived, about eight heathen [Tongvas] from a good village came to visit us; they live in this delightful place among the trees on the river."

—Father Juan Crespi, Spanish missionary, arriving at the Tongva village of Yangna, now Los Angeles, 1769.

and San Fernando, Rey de España, in 1797. Like other California missions, they were built on fertile land ideal for food production and grazing. The missions grew grain and had orchards of dates, olives, and other fruits. Their ranches raised sheep and cattle by the thousands and produced meat, candles, and leather. All the work was done by local Native people forced into labor by priests and soldiers who ran the missions. The missions prospered, selling their produce to traders who sailed along the coast.

Presidios and Pueblos

Four forts, called *presidios*, also scattered along the coast, protected the Spanish colony in California and its missions. To support these presidios, the Spanish founded several *pueblos*, or villages.

In 1779, Felipe de Neve, governor of California, began planning a pueblo between the two presidios of Santa Barbara and San Diego, near the Tongva village of Yangna. The Spanish government had offered land and supplies for farming to anyone who would settle in the pueblo and provide produce to the presidios.

Founding the Town

Recruiting settlers, or *pobladores*, for the new pueblo proved difficult. By August 1781, only eleven families had arrived at the San Gabriel Mission from Mexico.

Ethnically, the settlers were diverse. Of the eleven families, two were black, three were American Indian, two were Spanish men with American Indian wives, and the rest were a mix of the three. There were forty-four settlers altogether.

On September 4, 1781, Governor de Neve established the pueblo. Its official name was El Pueblo de la Reina de los Angeles ("The Village of the Queen of the Angels"), although many people think it was called El Pueblo de Nuestra Señora la Reina de los Angeles de Porciuncula ("The Village of Our Lady the Queen of the Angels of the Little Portion"). The town was named after the river that ran close by.

▼ *In its early days under Spanish and then Mexican rule, Los Angeles was a small pueblo. For many years afterward, it continued to look like a Mexican town.*

Angeles, and their Mexican owners, dominated the region for many years.

In 1830, Los Angeles still had only 770 Mexican residents. El Pueblo de Los Angeles was designated by Mexico as a city in 1835. Despite its lack of growth, it was actually the largest town in California until 1848. It had no specific industry of its own but served as a hub for the ranches surrounding it.

Los Angeles Joins the United States

White settlers from the United States, known as "Anglos" in California, began arriving in the region in the 1840s. In 1846, southern California became an area of conflict when hostility between Mexico and the United States erupted into war. The outcome of the war, which ended in 1848, was that the United States annexed vast areas of North America previously claimed by Mexico. California, and Los Angeles, then became part of the U.S.

From Pueblo to City

With just a few adobe houses and very narrow streets, the pueblo was small. Under Spanish rule, it remained a remote outpost and was slow to grow. In 1822, when Mexico gained its independence from Spain and became a nation in its own right, California became a Mexican province. Mexico dismantled the mission system, and the mission lands became private cattle ranches. The ranches surrounding Los

At the same time, large quantities of gold were found near what is now the city of Sacramento. The first official gold find had been made six years before, however, in the Placerita Canyon in Los Angeles County, and thousands of dollars' worth of gold was mined there over the next few years.

▼ *Many people from China came to California during the Gold Rush, and there was soon a strong Chinese community in Los Angeles. In this photo from 1903, a Chinese dragon joins the parade for the Mexican Fiesta de las Flores ("Feast of Flowers").*

California's population boomed, and in 1850, it became a state. Although Los Angeles was not the center of the Gold Rush, it was soon affected as more and more Anglos arrived to settle in southern California. Los Angeles became a violent place to live as fierce rivalry developed between Anglo settlers and Mexicans.

Development

From the 1870s on, several factors transformed Los Angeles into a booming U.S. city. In the mid-1800s, the town still

*"Hordes of Yankee emigrants . . .
are cultivating farms, establishing
vineyards, sawing up lumber, building
workshops, and doing a thousand things
which seem natural to them, but which
[Mexican] Californians neglect or
despise to do . . . . Shall these incursions
go unchecked until we shall become
strangers in our own land?"*

—Pío Pico,
last Mexican governor of California, 1846.

lacked a link with the East Coast, a water supply, a decent harbor, and a source of income. By the early 1900s, Los Angeles had all of these.

Things began to change in 1876 when a railroad from Los Angeles linked southern California to the eastern United States. With the railroad came settlers, and Los Angeles' population jumped from 5,700 in 1870 to more than 50,000 in 1890. Another 50,000 lived in the surrounding county where towns, orange groves, and farms—today part of the metropolitan area—sprang up.

Finding Oil and Building a Harbor

People had been drilling for oil around Los Angeles since the 1860s. The real boom started, however, in 1892 when evidence of oil was found downtown. Within a few years, two hundred companies had 2,500 oil wells operating within the city. Money and people flowed into the city along with the oil.

In 1899, development began on a small, shallow harbor in San Pedro, south of the city, to create a major seaport for Los Angeles. The shipping industry that developed as a result had a huge impact on the city's economy as large quantities of oil, agricultural produce, and manufactured products began to flow in and out of the port.

Boom in Population and Industry

These important developments over a short period of time transformed Los Angeles. A huge population boom started and continued at a fast pace. Land was gobbled up for housing and industry, and Los Angeles began the suburban spread that defines it today. By 1930, more than a million people lived in the city.

Piping in Water

With an average annual rainfall of about 15 inches (38 centimeters), Los Angeles has a constant problem with water supply. In 1913, William Mulholland built the longest aqueduct in the world, which piped drinking water 233 miles (375 kilometers) to Los Angeles from the Owens River Valley. It was later extended to 338 miles (544 km). Owens Valley residents and farmers opposed the project and dynamited the aqueduct several times in the 1920s.

Industry came to Los Angeles in the early 1900s, encouraged by a good seaport and cheap electricity supplied by the city. Because of its industries, Los Angeles was able to recover more quickly than most places from the Great Depression of the 1930s. Movies were one of the few businesses to flourish during the Depression, and the nation's young motion picture industry was based in Los Angeles. Another new industry, aircraft manufacturing, emerged during the 1920s and expanded greatly when the United States entered World War II in 1941.

Car Culture

World War II pulled the nation out of the Depression and Los Angeles experienced a surge of wealth in the 1950s. It was in this time that an important modern-day feature of L.A. life became dominant: the car. The

"Los Angeles was a place after my own heart. The people were hospitable. The country had the same attraction for me that it had for the Indians who originally chose this spot as their place to live . . . . It was so attractive to me that it at once became something about which my whole scheme of life was woven, I loved it so much."

—William Mulholland, self-trained engineer and builder of the Los Angeles Aqueduct.

"Los Angeles is a city on wheels, where [former president] Herbert Hoover's dream of 'two cars in every garage' nears fulfillment, even if 'two chickens in every pot' does not."

—Oliver Carlson, writer, 1941.

automobile had allowed for the development of suburbs since the 1920s, and commuting by car had become common in Los Angeles earlier than in other U.S. cities. By the 1940s and 1950s, the car had changed the face of the city: Garages were added onto houses; more and more roads were built; and gas stations opened by the hundreds. Car manufacturing around Los Angeles skyrocketed, and public transportation declined as everyone bought cars. Los Angeles' smog problem became part of life.

Into the Twenty-First Century

Although the manufacturing industry began to decline in the 1960s, other parts of the economy continued to flourish. The port, the entertainment and communication industries, local government, and the service and retail industries all expanded with the population. By 2003, the L.A. metropolitan region had a population of more than 17 million people.

▶ *As seen on Hollywood Boulevard, cars were already an important part of life in Los Angeles in the 1930s.*

CHAPTER 2

People of Los Angeles

Its huge size and agreeable climate are important factors in the character of Los Angeles, but it is the people, often called "Angelenos," who really make the city what it is. By the 1870s—more than twenty years after Los Angeles became part of the United States—not only Anglos but French, German, and Chinese people had joined the Mexican, African-American, Spanish, and Native American population. One hundred years later, people arrived in large numbers from Japan, Korea, Vietnam, Russia, Eastern and Western Europe, Latin America, and Canada.

In recent years, the city's population has actually become less diverse than it was—nearly half the residents are Latino (Hispanic), and most of those are of Mexican descent. Today in Los Angeles, most people speak Spanish or English or both, reflecting the dual Mexican-American heritage of the city.

A recent study at the University of California in Los Angeles (UCLA), however, identified 224 languages spoken in the county of Los Angeles. It also found there were locally produced publications in

◀ *A Japanese American drummer is ready to perform in the annual Nisei Week Parade in Little Tokyo.*

▶ The 2000 census shows that white people are the largest racial group in Los Angeles. Latinos, however, are by far the biggest ethnic group in Los Angeles. About 46.5 percent of the city's residents stated they were Latino. This is not considered a racial group, however, so most are classified in this chart as whites or "some other race."

180 of those languages, which means that those languages represent communities, however small.

Ethnic Communities

A number of ethnic communities in Los Angeles are anything but small: Los Angeles has the largest Asian and Latino populations in the United States. People in Los Angeles tend to live in their own ethnic groups. The wealthy suburbs are home to the large population of non-Latino white people. The South Central district is home to the majority of the city's African Americans, whose neighborhoods include Watts and Leimert Park. The shops and street cafés of Leimert Park Village have become something of a black cultural center, while the population of Watts now includes more Latinos than it does African

"A lot of people think there aren't any Indians in the San Fernando Valley anymore . . . . We have been here a long time and we plan to stay here."

—Rudy Ortega, Fernandeño Indian.

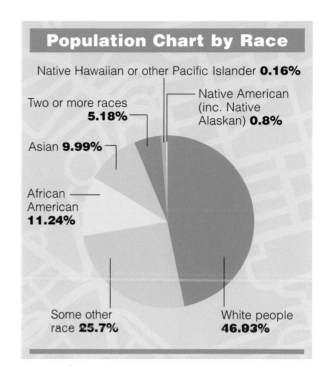

Population Chart by Race

Native Hawaiian or other Pacific Islander **0.16%**

Native American (inc. Native Alaskan) **0.8%**

Two or more races **5.18%**

Asian **9.99%**

African American **11.24%**

Some other race **25.7%**

White people **46.93%**

Americans. East Los Angeles, just outside the city, is a Latino center, but there are many Latino communities dotted throughout the city, too.

There are a number of strong Asian communities that reflect immigration to the city at different periods—Chinatown, Little Tokyo, Koreatown, and the Vietnamese neighborhood in Lincoln Heights. Los Angeles County has more Native Americans than any other county in the United States, and they represent over one hundred tribes.

Immigrants

Of Los Angeles' nearly 3.9 million residents, more than a million are not U.S. citizens. What lies behind that extraordinary figure? Los Angeles has a huge number of Mexican

The Korean Community

Over 90,000 Korean Americans live in Los Angeles. They have established Koreatown in the downtown area as their business center, although most of them live elsewhere. Their traditional religion is Buddhism, but there are now hundreds of Korean Protestant churches in the metropolitan region. The Korean residents of Los Angeles have a reputation for being hardworking owners of small businesses. This has sometimes caused conflicts in poor, black neighborhoods where Koreans have bought many grocery stores and gas stations from African Americans.

▲ L.A. Dodgers' pitcher Kazuhisa Ishii coaches baseball in a community program in Koreatown.

immigrants, and many of them choose to live there illegally rather than return to Mexico and face worse poverty than they experience in the United States.

Immigration is a hugely controversial issue in Los Angeles. Some people say that poverty-stricken illegal immigrants are a drain on the educational, welfare, and health systems. Others point out that most newcomers fulfill a vital role in the city, because they are prepared to take low-income jobs in factories and services.

A positive aspect of Los Angeles' ethnic diversity is that a variety of nationalities, religions, and customs makes for a lively, exciting city. The negative side is that racial and ethnic mistrust and hostility have created a great divide that expresses itself not just in inequality but also in violence and crime.

▼ Community members get together to clean up after the 1992 riots.

Gangs

Los Angeles gangs, divided by ethnic origin, have existed for many years. Many feel that their involvement in drugs and violence since the late 1960s reflects the hopelessness of neighborhoods where unemployment is high and drug abuse has taken hold. Of the estimated four hundred gangs and more than sixty thousand gang members, about half are Latino. The Bloods and the Crips are African-American gangs that have been

Race Riots

Los Angeles has been the site of several major riots. The seeds of the riots lay in racial mistrust, a problem that persists in the city today. The first riot was the Chinese Massacre of 1871. A mob of about five hundred white people killed nineteen Chinese men and boys. In June 1943, the Zoot Suit Riots were a culmination of conflict between white sailors and soldiers and Mexican and black youths. The servicemen rounded up and beat their victims, whom the police did nothing to help. In 1965, approximately one thousand people were injured and thirty-four killed in the Watts Riot—six days of looting and burning. A period of intense racial tension preceded the riot, which was triggered when two white patrol officers arrested an African American man. In 1992, one of the nation's worst riots, resulting in fifty-five deaths, started in protest at the unpunished beating of an African American man by white police officers.

▲ *A multiethnic group of boy scouts in Los Angeles participate in a Memorial Day service.*

around since the 1970s. Former rivals, they signed a pact after the 1992 riots. There are over thirty Asian gangs as well as a few white gangs. Gang members wear caps, jackets, or sweatbands that identify them, and they often carry weapons.

A City of Many Faiths

The residents of Los Angeles practice many religions. The Roman Catholic faith dominates, because it is the main religion of immigrants from Latin America. Roman Catholics have been in the city since its first

days, but since then, the arrival of Asians, Africans, and non-Latino whites have brought a variety of religions to Los Angeles. Protestants, Muslims, and Jews all have places of worship in the city, and people from Asian countries have introduced the eastern religions of Buddhism and Hinduism. In recent years, the descendants of the Tongva people, who were all but wiped out by Spanish, Mexican, and Anglo settlers, have revived their ancient faith and are protecting the Tongvas' ancient, sacred sites.

Festivals

Los Angeles has many festivals, both religious and nonreligious. One of the most ancient is the 1,500-year-old Oban Festival, a Buddhist holiday observed in the city's temples. The Chinese and Japanese communities in Los Angeles date back to the 1800s, and both the Chinese New Year and Japanese New Year have long been celebrated in the city.

Apart from the traditional celebrations that can be found in other cities and countries, there are a few festivals that are more particular to the people of Los Angeles. La Fiesta de Los Angeles, also called Fiesta de las Flores ("Feast of Flowers"), was first held in 1894 to celebrate the city's Latino heritage. It is now held on Broadway, a major shopping district for many Latinos, as part of the annual Cinco de Mayo celebrations in the city. The Watts Summer Festival is a three-day celebration of African-American culture that also aims to encourage community pride. Nisei Week began in 1935 to attract business and goodwill to the Little Tokyo neighborhood and now celebrates Japanese-American culture.

▶ Mexican-American musicians perform at the Cinco de Mayo celebrations in downtown Los Angeles.

CHAPTER 3

Living in Los Angeles

"Los Angeles is seventy-two suburbs in search of a city."

—Dorothy Parker, writer and humorist.

To get a sense of what it is like to live in Los Angeles, you have to imagine a suburban community of stores, malls, public facilities, parking lots, houses, and apartment buildings that seem to go on forever. As one community melts into another, there are often no clear dividing lines. Some neighborhoods, however, are more varied; the landscape changes from flat to hilly, or the neighborhoods change from posh to poor.

Getting Around

This vast urban sprawl means that life in Los Angeles is based around the automobile. The first freeway in the metropolitan area (now the Pasadena Freeway) opened in 1939, and a huge freeway system was built between 1947 and 1970. Today, the multilane freeways crisscross the city and surrounding region. Every day, the network is choked with several million commuters, shoppers, and visitors.

◄ *Vehicles whiz through an interchange in Los Angeles' huge freeway system.*

▲ Cars fill the street on a busy stretch of Sunset Boulevard. Automobiles are the main reason for Los Angeles' pollution problem.

There is a public bus system in Los Angeles, but it is used by only about 10 percent of the city's 1.5 million commuters. A rail system, the Metro Rail, has recently been built to connect Los Angeles and other communities in the county and metropolitan areas. The first line opened in 1990 with little impact on traffic congestion, but eventually it may help ease the problem.

Downtown

In spite of its image as an endless suburb, Los Angeles has had a downtown area since its earliest days. The old pueblo district, the current business district, the markets and wholesale districts, City Hall, and the Pacific Stock Exchange are all downtown.

Sunset Boulevard

One of the older arteries of the city, Sunset Boulevard runs for 25 miles (40 km) through L.A., connecting the downtown to the Pacific Ocean. It passes through several neighborhoods, each imprinting its section of Sunset Boulevard with a different character. The boulevard starts near Olvera Street, in the original part of the city. It winds through Hollywood, where many of the original movie studios were. Most are now television studios. In West Hollywood, Sunset Boulevard becomes Sunset Strip, 1.5 miles (2.4 km) of restaurants and music clubs that are the center of Los Angeles' nightlife. Sunset Boulevard changes character completely as it enters Beverly Hills, a luxurious residential neighborhood, which sits in the middle of L.A. but is not part of it. The road ends up in the seaside neighborhood of the Pacific Palisades.

Housing and other buildings in Los Angeles have traditionally been built low. From 1905 to 1957, there was a ban on buildings higher than 150 feet or thirteen stories tall, the only exception being the twenty-eight-story City Hall. Originally introduced to prevent the city from looking like New York's Manhattan, the height limit also reduced the threat of damage during earthquakes. The ban also encouraged the city to spread outward into large suburbs of one-story houses. The lifting of the ban and new technology allowed for the construction of steel-framed skyscrapers in the 1960s and 1970s, changing the face of downtown Los Angeles.

Housing

Housing varies according to the neighborhood—it ranges from the billionaires' mansions of Bel-Air to the crowded apartment buildings of South-Central Los Angeles. At one end of the social scale, Los Angeles has many wealthy neighborhoods where swimming pools and large houses abound. Increasingly, these are gated communities, with security guards posted to prevent nonresidents from driving or walking in.

▼ *Houses and palm trees perch on the hillsides in the Hollywood Hills neighborhood.*

After World War II, there was an explosive housing boom as the city expanded and tens of thousands of inexpensive, one-story houses were built. Two Los Angeles housing styles, the bungalows of the early 1900s and the post-war ranch house, later spread all over the United States. It has been claimed that by 1980, Los Angeles had more private houses than any other city in the world. Since the 1990s, due to lack of space, more apartments and condominiums have been built.

More than half the city's residents live in rented houses or apartments. Rental prices have soared beyond many people's means. Overcrowding has become a problem in poor districts, and there is an acute housing shortage for low-income people living in Los Angeles. The city's public housing projects in South Central, and similar projects in East Los Angeles, have waiting lists of many thousands.

Homelessness

Like other California cities, Los Angeles has a considerable population of homeless people—it is impossible to give an accurate figure, but it numbers in the thousands. Among these are the invisible homeless: poverty-stricken families living in motels or cars because they do not have the means to

▶ Churches are active in the run-down area of Skid Row, running modern-day missions that provide beds and food. These people are eating a Christmas meal at a Los Angeles mission for homeless people.

Skid Row

A fifty-block area of downtown Los Angeles known as Skid Row has the largest concentration of homeless people in the United States. Some of them live in shelters made of cardboard boxes, and others sleep on the sidewalk in tents or in the open air. There are also many cheap hotels and overnight shelters that specifically cater to homeless people. City officials are trying to address homelessness and drug addiction by keeping people from sleeping on sidewalks and getting tough on petty criminals, but the problems are still increasing.

"Homelessness is an unsolvable dilemma. In my twenty-nine years here, I'm convinced not much can be done. All we can do is help the few that want it and give comfort to those who need it."

—Clancy Imislund, director of the Midnight Mission and former homeless person on Skid Row, quoted by Charlie LeDuff, *The New York Times*, July 2003.

rent an apartment. Other homeless people are more obvious, because they live on the streets, victims of mental illness or addictions to drugs and alcohol.

Crime

Drug and alcohol abuse not only cause homelessness but are behind much of the crime in U.S. cities. Alcohol and drugs trigger violence, and in addition, many thefts are by people desperate for money to feed their drug addiction. Crime in Los Angeles—once considered the murder capital of the United States—is down since its peak in the early 1990s, but it continues to color everyday life. Car thefts hover at about one hundred a day. In poorer and gang-dominated neighborhoods, street crimes such as fighting, vandalism, drug dealing, and mugging are more of a threat.

Living with the Environment

On some days, when the city is blanketed under a cloud of noxious gases, the air pollution in Los Angeles is very unpleasant to live with and dangerous to people's health. Factories and other businesses that create pollution are fined if they cause too much pollution, but emissions from the city's huge numbers of vehicles are the main cause. In addition, the mountains that surround L.A. trap air over the city and prevent the smog from being blown away by sea breezes. Much has already been done to address the problem of vehicle emissions. Public transportation is making a comeback after many years; carpooling is encouraged; and car emissions are strictly controlled. The air in Los Angeles is dramatically cleaner than it was twenty years ago, although Los Angeles remains one of the nation's three smoggiest cities.

Earthquakes

People in Los Angeles are used to living with earthquakes—the last large quake was

▲ Sixteen people died when this apartment building collapsed in the severe Northridge earthquake of 1994.

- *Remain calm—do not panic.*
- *Remain where you are.*
- *Indoors . . . . get under heavy furniture or huddle against an inside wall. Cover face and head.*
- *Outdoors, stay away from buildings, trees, and power lines.*
- *In a car, stop at the side of the road… Stay in the car until the earthquake is over.*

—Advice on how to survive an earthquake from a Los Angeles County pamphlet.

in 1994, but little tremors occur frequently. Even though many newer buildings exceed the old height limit, they are constructed to resist earthquakes. The new buildings are designed with frames that are flexible, helping them to absorb the shaking. Others are built so solid that they withstand the earthquake and stay in one piece.

Problems with Water

Water, and the lack of it, is still a problem in Los Angeles. The Santa Monica Bay, on which Los Angeles sits, has become very polluted by the region's development. The waterways and beaches are polluted by trash, sewage, chemicals, industrial waste, and other debris, killing marine life and spoiling beaches for swimmers and surfers.

Los Angeles' long-running battle to provide enough water for its residents shows no sign of coming to an end. The city uses about 150 gallons (568 liters) per person a day in spite of a successful awareness program that has introduced some conservation measures. The city offers financial incentives to people who install water-efficient appliances in their homes. It also has developed irrigation systems that do not waste water and programs to help businesses use less water. On average, 50 percent of L.A.'s water comes through the L.A. Aqueduct. Local groundwater supplies 15 percent and the metropolitan Water District of Southern California—a water importer and wholesaler—provides the deficit.

Shopping

In spite of their city's problems, Los Angeles residents go about their daily life— shopping, going to school and college, and earning a living. Most people shop as they do elsewhere in the United States: in large, inexpensive chain stores in their neighborhoods. The city's ethnic mix and the enormous wealth of a few of its residents, however, create opportunities for some out-of-the-ordinary stores. Los Angeles' richer residents and tourists head for Rodeo Drive in Beverly Hills, which has several blocks of staggeringly expensive boutiques. Those in

search of bargains head for an area of downtown Los Angeles where there are many clothes manufacturers. The area, which has recently been named the "Fashion District," has become one of the city's most crowded and popular shopping districts.

Going to School

More than half of the city's school-age students speak Spanish, and for many of them, studying in English is a struggle. The language problems are not confined to Spanish-speaking students—it is estimated that city students speak any of about ninety different languages when they are at home with their families. A California law says that schools with many non-English speaking students must offer to teach children in their native language if parents wish it. About 10 percent of students in the Los Angeles School district are taught in their native language and also study English for two hours a day.

Meanwhile, public schools in Los Angeles are very short of money and have the lowest ratio of teachers to students in the nation. Combined with the language barriers, the overcrowding of classrooms may account for a decline in achievement among Los Angeles schools. Most children from high-income families are sent to private schools to avoid the problems.

The Colleges

Los Angeles is home to two top U.S. colleges. The University of Southern

California (USC), opened in 1880, is the oldest private university in the western states. It has excellent law and medical schools and an outstanding sports program. No other university has won as many sports championships as USC. Sixteen percent of USC's students in 2003 came from 155 countries around the world, and the rest were from the United States.

UCLA, the largest branch of the University of California with 37,000 students, is academically renowned. The campus covers 400 acres (162 hectares), and includes the UCLA Medical Center, a hospital with a worldwide reputation. UCLA has a major film school and is an important research center—the Internet was launched there in 1969—with more than 280 research departments, institutes, and laboratories.

▼ *Students take a break on the UCLA campus. Most of UCLA's undergraduates are from California.*

CHAPTER 4

Los Angeles at Work

The residents of Los Angeles are represented by a mayor, a city attorney, a controller, and a fifteen-member city council. On behalf of the citizens, these elected officials head the city government and make decisions about how to run Los Angeles. The government is based at City Hall downtown.

The mayor is the equivalent, at the city level, of a president, and he shares his powers in many areas with the council. The council members are like members of congress, each representing one district but working together to make decisions and pass laws. They also have areas of special responsibility, such as city planning, public safety, or the budget. The county attorney has two roles: to look after the city's legal affairs and to be the prosecutor in court cases. The controller is in charge of the city's financial accounts. The city also has a number of commissions—groups of people who oversee specific departments, such as the Port of Los Angeles department, or who advise the mayor and council on subjects ranging from cultural heritage to child care.

◄ *The Los Angeles Harbor brings more than 200,000 jobs to the metropolitan area, and international trade is one of the largest industries in Los Angeles County.*

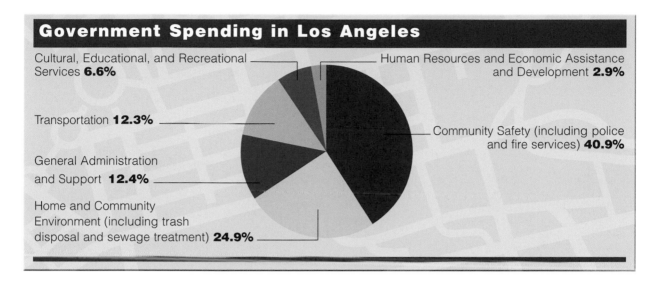

Government Spending in Los Angeles

Cultural, Educational, and Recreational Services **6.6%**

Transportation **12.3%**

General Administration and Support **12.4%**

Home and Community Environment (including trash disposal and sewage treatment) **24.9%**

Human Resources and Economic Assistance and Development **2.9%**

Community Safety (including police and fire services) **40.9%**

Paying for Services

The city's workers are part of a network that includes everyone from firefighters, community workers, and librarians to the many people who maintain the city's infrastructure. The city has more than forty-five thousand full-time employees, and that costs a lot of money. Los Angeles residents pay for the city's employees and services

▲ *The largest chunk of taxpayers' money in Los Angeles—40.9 cents of every dollar—was spent on community safety in 2000–2001. Of that sum, 27.1 cents of every tax dollar was spent on crime control.*

▼ *A worker with the L.A. Department of Water and Power inspects a pipe on the Los Angeles Aqueduct.*

through taxes, but the money raised is never enough. Because of a 1978 California law called Proposition 13, which lowered property taxes and limited other taxation on residents, Los Angeles has had to cut back on services to save money.

"In a great city, City Hall must be a beacon to the people's aspirations."

—Tom Bradley, mayor of Los Angeles from 1973 to 1993.

▲ *City Hall, the tall building, is part of the Civic Center, which houses thousands of government workers.*

The Business District
City Hall is part of a government complex—one of the world's largest—called the Civic Center. The center contains offices not just for city employees but for county, state, and federal workers, too. The Civic Center is next to the "old" downtown area, where the business and shopping center of Los Angeles was until about 1945.

The First Policewoman

The United States' first policewoman was Alice Stebbins Wells, a former social worker in Los Angeles. She was appointed to the Los Angeles Police Department on September 12, 1910. Her duties were wide ranging, from looking for missing persons and enforcing laws in recreational facilities to "suppression of unwholesome billboard displays." Wells' appointment was publicized nationwide, and she herself promoted the need for female police officers. By 1916, sixteen other U.S. cities had policewomen.

By the 1960s, there were shopping areas throughout the city, and the business district had shifted to "new" downtown, or the Central Business District. In its two hundred or so blocks, looming skyscrapers

▼ *This chart shows the variety of occupations of men and women in Los Angeles.*

house the usual businesses found in such districts: banks and other financial services, the headquarters of large companies, real estate offices, and law and accounting firms. Thousands of people commute to work in downtown Los Angeles offices every day.

Manufacturing Industry

The boom in aircraft production during World War II led to a long-term industry for Los Angeles. The aerospace industry produces missiles, aircraft, spacecraft, and their communication systems and instruments. Although the industry has declined from its height in the 1970s, it still accounts for about one-fourth of manufacturing jobs in Los Angeles.

America's Largest Port

Los Angeles Harbor, as in its earliest days, continues to bring huge wealth to Los Angeles. In combination with neighboring Long Beach Harbor, Worldport L.A. (as it is

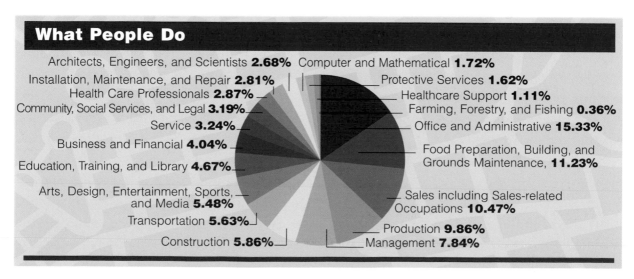

What People Do

- Architects, Engineers, and Scientists **2.68%**
- Installation, Maintenance, and Repair **2.81%**
- Health Care Professionals **2.87%**
- Community, Social Services, and Legal **3.19%**
- Service **3.24%**
- Business and Financial **4.04%**
- Education, Training, and Library **4.67%**
- Arts, Design, Entertainment, Sports, and Media **5.48%**
- Transportation **5.63%**
- Construction **5.86%**
- Computer and Mathematical **1.72%**
- Protective Services **1.62%**
- Healthcare Support **1.11%**
- Farming, Forestry, and Fishing **0.36%**
- Office and Administrative **15.33%**
- Food Preparation, Building, and Grounds Maintenance, **11.23%**
- Sales including Sales-related Occupations **10.47%**
- Production **9.86%**
- Management **7.84%**

now officially called) is the third largest port in the world. Automobiles, fuel, and metals are among its main imports, but it is very likely that several items in your home, such as toys or shoes, came through the port in Los Angeles. Over half of its trade comes from East Asia, and Los Angeles' vast economy is increasingly tied to the Pacific Rim countries.

Manufacturing as a whole provides many thousands of jobs in Los Angeles. The 1992 economic census recorded more than 28,000 factories in the metropolitan area, which makes it one of the top production regions in the United States. The factories make everything from clothing and furniture to electronic equipment and heavy machinery.

Agriculture and Day Workers

The large and ever-growing group in Los Angeles known as the "working poor" is mostly Latinos, many of them illegal immigrants. Thousands gather every day at a few recognized spots throughout the city. They are day laborers, and the lucky ones will be chosen by employers looking for temporary help on farms or in factories. The working poor are also restaurant and hotel workers, maids, gardeners, janitors, and hospital support workers.

Surprisingly, considering its huge urban population, California is still an agricultural region. Several thousand people in the city earn their living at the Los Angeles Wholesale Produce Market and the 19th Street Market, which together make up the

"Los Angeles is a place built on imagination. Its creative energy is keeping the economy going."

—George Huang, economist, Los Angeles County Economic Development Corporation, August 2003.

world's second largest wholesale produce market (New York has the largest). Every day, fresh produce is brought into the heart of the city on trucks and sold at auction.

The Entertainment Industries

If Los Angeles were famous for one thing only, it would be for its role as the center of the motion picture industry. Since the first studio opened in 1906, the industry has grown with the city and was once (in the 1920s and 1930s) the city's main employer. Some of the studios and other movie-based businesses from the old days still exist in Hollywood, but the movie industry is now scattered throughout Los Angeles County and is very different than it was in its earlier days. The ever-increasing power of television means that movies are made today by huge business conglomerates rather than independent film studios, and even box-office blockbusters are just one small part of the vast entertainment and media industry. Los Angeles, however, has remained a base for all this growth and for American popular culture. Since the 1970s, Los Angeles has also been the center for the world's music recording industry, and it has more radio stations than any other city.

▲ *Members of this television film crew are on location filming an episode of "Baywatch."*

In spite of all this media activity, only a small percentage of workers in Los Angeles are directly employed as professionals in the arts, entertainment, and media sectors. The city is, however, home to thousands of hopeful musicians and actors working in other jobs and waiting for their big break.

CHAPTER 5

Los Angeles at Play

Much of life in Los Angeles, especially recreational life, is lived outdoors. From sports to eating to listening to music, a lot of the things people do to have fun in Los Angeles take place in the open air.

Heading to the Beaches

Beach life is the most obvious example of the city's outdoor lifestyle. There are miles of coastline and sandy beaches within reach of the city, and they are used for swimming, surfing, boating, fishing, and beach sports. On weekends, city dwellers find their way to the beach communities, where parking lots and side streets overflow with visitors' cars. As many as half a million people have been recorded on the beaches of Los Angeles County in one day. Surfing is especially popular in southern California. The beaches of Malibu, next to Los Angeles, are famous for their large waves.

Open Spaces

The largest municipal park in the United States is L.A.'s Griffith Park, which covers 5 square miles (13 square km). Although part of the city, it also stretches into the

◀ Venice Beach is one of Los Angeles' most popular recreation spots with both city residents and visitors.

Venice

The beach community of Venice—both the place itself and the people who flock there—reflects Los Angeles' eccentricity and originality. Modeled on the Italian city of the same name and built around a network of canals, Venice opened as a recreational spot in 1905. The community went through a decline, but since the 1970s, houses have been restored and expensive shops and restaurants have appeared. The oceanfront in Venice attracts crowds in search of amusement or just a stroll along the boardwalk to watch bodybuilders and volleyball players on the beach. The boardwalk is famous for its street performers and stalls bursting with exotic items.

local mountains. Its hillsides are covered in the native brush and low trees, such as sagebrush and scrub oak, that is called "chaparral." Wild animals—skunks, deer, rattlesnakes, and hawks— live in the park, and it is also home to the Los Angeles Zoo. Griffith Park has four golf courses and miles of hiking and riding trails. There are about 350 other public parks throughout the city.

Sports

Los Angeles also has more than 150 recreation centers for sports and other

▼ *Griffith Observatory, opened in 1935, is one of Griffith Park's main attractions. Visitors can enjoy shows in the planetarium or look at scientific curiosities in the Hall of Science.*

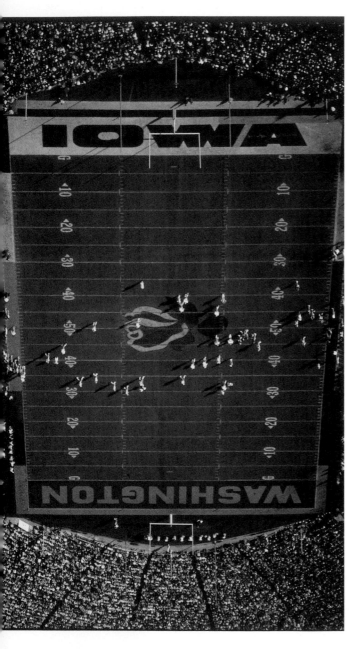

▲ Crowds pack the Rose Bowl for the championship game on New Year's Day.

Los Angeles Sports Teams	
Baseball	Dodgers
	Anaheim Angels
Basketball (NBA)	Lakers
	Clippers
Basketball (WNBA)	Sparks
Football	Trojans (USC)
	Bruins (UCLA)
Hockey	Kings
Soccer	Galaxy

activities, and there are endless opportunities for outside recreational sports. The climate is well suited to bicycling, hiking, and jogging. In-line skaters cruise along streets, and outdoor basketball games are played everywhere. The city has twelve golf courses, and there are twenty more in the surrounding county.

Spectator sports are as important in Los Angeles as they are in the rest of the United States. Los Angeles is home to the legendary basketball team the Lakers, who have won the NBA championship many times, most recently in 2000, 2001, and 2002.

Baseball fans in the Los Angeles area have two teams they can support—the Los Angeles Dodgers and the Anaheim Angels, based in Orange County. The Dodgers last won the World Series in 1988. The Angels, on the other hand, won their first World Series in 2002.

Strangely, Los Angeles has had no professional football team since 1995 when the Raiders moved back to Oakland and the Rams moved to St. Louis. Luckily for football fans, college football thrives in the city. USC football teams yield more

professionals annually than any other college in the United States. UCLA's home field is the Rose Bowl in Pasadena. There, every year on New Year's Day, the Rose Bowl hosts championship football, pitting two of the nation's top college teams against one another. The game is accompanied by the spectacular Tournament of Roses, one of the world's most famous New Year's Day parades. Several Super Bowls and the 1994 World Cup soccer championship have also taken place at the Rose Bowl.

Performing Arts

As well as being the world's largest center of mass entertainment, Los Angeles is a city of considerable artistic achievement. Orchestras, theaters, operas, and the visual arts flourish in the city's creative atmosphere.

▲ *The new home for the Los Angeles Philharmonic— the Walt Disney Concert Hall—was designed by Frank Gehry and opened in 2003.*

The Los Angeles Philharmonic is one of the world's major orchestras. It performs all over the world, but when at home, the orchestra often plays to local audiences at the Hollywood Bowl. Up to 250,000 people listen to the philharmonic's "Symphonies Under the Stars" every summer. The Los Angeles Chamber Orchestra is the city's other major orchestra.

At one time, Los Angeles was the only large U.S. city with no professional opera company. In 1986, an opera company, Los Angeles Opera, was founded that has flourished and now boasts the famous singer Plácido Domingo as its artistic director.

Looking Forward

For years, people have talked of the "Big One," an earthquake of 8.0 or more on the Richter scale. It could happen at any time, causing immense loss of life and damage in Los Angeles. Nevertheless, people continue to pour into Los Angeles, putting pressure on natural resources and public services.

Dealing with the Water Shortage

As a water deficit looms in the near future, Los Angeles has to find new ways of providing water. One possibility is desalination, or taking the salt out of seawater to make it drinkable. A 2002 report to the California legislature, based on Los Angeles' water needs, urged the state to introduce desalination plants.

Dealing with Transportation

Ground transportation policies in Los Angeles aim to decrease traffic congestion, conserve fuel, and keep down levels of pollution. The Metro Rail is still expanding through the metropolitan area, and a growing number of lanes on the freeway are kept exclusively for carpoolers. The message to commuters is that if they cut down on fuel and car usage, they will get to

◄ *Homeless survivors wait to be allocated shelters after the 1994 earthquake. Both the city and county of Los Angeles teach people how to prepare for earthquakes and what to do during one.*

▲ It is hoped that the Metro Rail will help ease traffic congestion and pollution in the greater metropolitan area of Los Angeles. This is the North Hollywood Metro Rail station on the day it opened in 2000.

work faster. Every year, more people are avoiding transportation problems altogether by working at home.

L.A. 2000

In 1988, the City of Los Angeles released a report titled, "L.A. 2000: A City for the Future," addressing its future challenges. These issues included maintaining livable communities and a decent environment, improving transportation, sustaining the city's diversity, and maintaining adequate funding and government.

Much progress has been made in many of those areas since the report was written. The crime rate began to drop steeply in the mid-1990s, partly due to the improvement and expansion of the police department. Air pollution has dropped equally dramatically.

A new subway system has been built, and there are big plans to expand Los Angeles International Airport, already one of the world's busiest airports. In addition, the city's ethnic groups have demanded and received increasing recognition.

Future Challenges

In spite of all the progress, the issues facing Los Angeles are still the same as they were when the L.A. 2000 report was issued. This is partly because the population continues to increase, and partly because all California governments face budget deficits. Proposition 13 limits the powers of state and local governments in California to raise taxes, and so the L.A. city government has to cut its services. Everything suffers, from health care and education to environmental and cultural programs.

Yet, Los Angeles is leading the world in its attempt to create a truly equal multiethnic society. With its unique mix of people, it is already a city of the future.